I0039044

the Journey to Centennial

PASSPORT

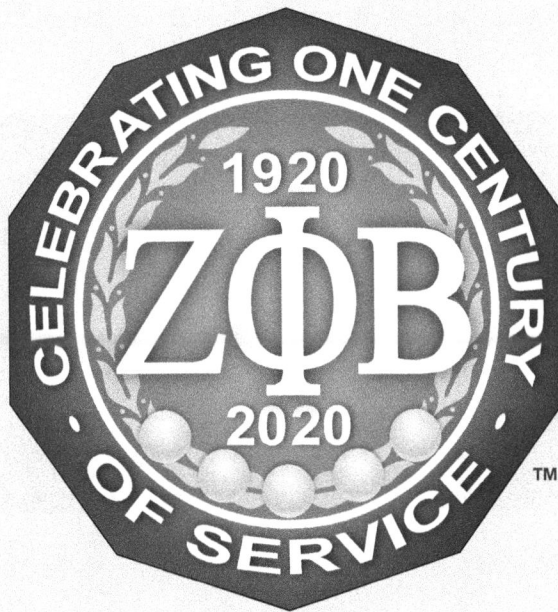

ZETA PHI BETA SORORITY, INCORPORATED

ZETA PHI BETA SORORITY, INCORPORATED

ESTABLISHED
JANUARY 16, 1920

ZETA PHI BETA SORORITY, INCORPORATED

SCHOLARSHIP – SERVICE – SISTERHOOD – FINER WOMANHOOD

"In the beginning, the five of us,

Viola Tyler, Myrtle Tyler,

Pearl Neal, Fannie Pettie, and

myself did whatever

our hands found to do."

Founder Arizona Cleaver Stemons, 1920

How fortunate to be a Soror whose chapter was organized by one of the "Five Pearls"!

Founder Fannie Pettie Watts, 1949

January 16, 2015

My Dear Soror,

I am excited that you have obtained your PASSPORT to join sorors, globally, as we embark upon our historical *Journey to Centennial!*

We will blaze new paths to commemorate our founding in 1920 and there will be many opportunities to capture this once-in-a-lifetime journey. It is my hope that each stamp in your PASSPORT will remind you of our Founders' vision as we lift their legacy of Service, Scholarship, Sisterhood and Finer Womanhood.

Let *the Journey to Centennial* begin!

For the Love of Zeta,

Mary Breaux Wright

Mary Breaux Wright
24th International Grand Basileus

"Thanks to God for permitting
me to see this day
(40th Anniversary Celebration).
This is a day for rejoicing
for past successes and looking
to the future for higher hills to
climb in service. God give us hills!
And strength for climbing."

Founder Pearl A. Neal, 1960

ZETA PHI BETA SORORITY, INCORPORATED

OFFICIAL
CENTENNIAL PASSPORT

PERSONAL DATA:

Name..
<<<<<<<<<<<<<<<<<<<<<<<<<<<<<<<<<<<<<<<<

Initiating
Chapter..
<<<<<<<<<<<<<<<<<<<<<<<<<<<<<<<<<<<<<<<<

City/State...
<<<<<<<<<<<<<<<<<<<<<<<<<<<<<<<<<<<<<<<<

Initiating Date/Year.......................................
<<<<<<<<<<<<<<<<<<<<<<<<<<<<<<<<<<<<<<<<

Grand Basileus
During
Initiating Year..
<<<<<<<<<<<<<<<<<<<<<<<<<<<<<<<<<<<<<<<<

Current Chapter..
<<<<<<<<<<<<<<<<<<<<<<<<<<<<<<<<<<<<<<<<

City/State...
<<<<<<<<<<<<<<<<<<<<<<<<<<<<<<<<<<<<<<<<

Centennial
Visionaries
Number
<<<<<<<<<<<<<<<<<<<<<<<<<<<<<<<<<<<<<<<<

CENTENNIAL PASSPORT
INSTRUCTIONS

This PASSPORT has been officially licensed by Zeta Phi Beta Sorority, Incorporated's Centennial Commission and should only be used by members of Zeta Phi Beta Sorority. This PASSPORT may be obtained at designated Sorority events through 2020 and online at Amazon. You must be present at the event to receive the stamp.

Members may create and purchase their own stamps to commemorate an event or personal brand through the official *Centennial Passport Project*. For more information on creating or purchasing a stamp for your *Centennial Passport Experience*, contact: centennialpassport2020@gmail.com

Stamp and/or sticker originators, please register all PASSPORT stamps and/or stickers at the official Centennial Website: www.zphib2020.com

WELCOME TO
"THE JOURNEY TO CENTENNIAL"

The Journey to Centennial officially launched on Friday, January 9, 2015 at the National Executive Board Meeting. Our journey concludes at the National Executive Board Meeting in January 2021.

There are poignant, pivotal and provocative questions that we must ask along this journey. THINK about:

- What will I do to "Be Finer in 2020"?
- Where will I travel to capture and record memories of my journey?
- Who will I connect with as I travel the highways reflected in "The House by the Side of the Road"?
- When will I experience my transformation as a next level community conscious, action-oriented member?
- How will Zeta be a stronger organization because of my personal commitment to Service, Scholarship, Sisterhood and Finer Womanhood?

Capture your personal mile-markers in this PASSPORT on your *Journey to Centennial*. It is going to be the trip of a lifetime!

Dr. Jylla Moore Tearte
20th International Grand Basileus
Centennial Commission Chair

"I have a profound admiration and respect for those of you who have worked and built the fine structure upon the foundation laid in 1920: A structure whose fundamental principles are Sisterly Love, Service, Scholarship, and Finer Womanhood."

Founder Myrtle Tyler Faithful, 1960

"A Zeta is a girl, regardless

of race, creed or color, who has

high standards and principles,

a good scholarly average

and an active interest in all things

that she undertakes to accomplish."

Founder Viola Tyler Goings, circa 1920-1930

the Journey to Centennial PASSPORT

CELEBRATING ONE CENTURY OF SERVICE
1920 ZΦB 2020

Archonian Club

ZΦB

DATE: _____

EVENT: _____

MOMENT TO REMEMBER: _____

_____

_____

_____

_____

_____

AFFIX STAMP HERE

_____

_____

_____

_____

_____

_____

_____

_____

_____

PASSPORT

the Journey to Centennial

CELEBRATING ONE CENTURY
1920 ZΦB 2020
OF SERVICE

AFFIX STAMP HERE

DATE: ....

EVENT: ....

MOMENT TO REMEMBER: ....

....

....

....

....

....

....

....

....

....

....

....

....

....

....

2

<<<<<< ZETA PHI BETA SORORITY, INC.
<<<<<<<<<<<<<<<<<<<<<<<<<<<<<<<<<<<

the Journey to Centennial PASSPORT

CELEBRATING ONE CENTURY OF SERVICE
ZΦB 1920 2020

DATE: ....

EVENT: ....

MOMENT TO REMEMBER: ....

AFFIX STAMP HERE

PASSPORT

the Journey to
Centennial

CELEBRATING ONE CENTURY
1920
ZΦB
2020
OF SERVICE

AFFIX STAMP HERE

DATE:

EVENT:

MOMENT TO REMEMBER:

<<<<<< ZETA PHI BETA SORORITY, INC.
<<<<<<<<<<<<<<<<<<<<<<<<<<<<<<<

CELEBRATING ONE CENTURY OF SERVICE
ZΦB
1920 2020

DATE: _____

EVENT: _____

MOMENT TO REMEMBER: _____

_____

_____

_____

_____

_____

_____

_____

_____

_____

_____

_____

_____

_____

_____

AFFIX STAMP HERE

"No Greek-letter organization has a greater movement than ours—'Finer Womanhood'."
- Soror Venetia E. Nichols, 1928

PASSPORT

the Journey to *Centennial*

CELEBRATING ONE CENTURY
1920
ZΦB
2020
OF SERVICE

AFFIX STAMP HERE

DATE:_____

EVENT:_____

MOMENT TO REMEMBER:_____

_____

_____

_____

_____

_____

_____

_____

_____

_____

_____

_____

_____

_____

_____

_____

<<<<<< ZETA PHI BETA SORORITY, INC.
<<<<<<<<<<<<<<<<<<<<<<<<<<<<<<<

the Journey to Centennial PASSPORT

CELEBRATING ONE CENTURY OF SERVICE
ZΦB 1920 2020

DATE: ....

EVENT: ....

MOMENT TO REMEMBER: ....

AFFIX STAMP HERE

ZETA PHI BETA SORORITY, INC. <<<<<<
<<<<<<<<<<<<<<<<<<<<<<<<<<<<<<<<<<<<

7

PASSPORT

the Journey to **Centennial**

CELEBRATING ONE CENTURY OF SERVICE
1920 ZΦB 2020

AFFIX STAMP HERE

DATE: _____

EVENT: _____

MOMENT TO REMEMBER: _____

_____

_____

_____

_____

_____

_____

_____

_____

_____

_____

_____

_____

_____

_____

<<<<<< ZETA PHI BETA SORORITY, INC.
<<<<<<<<<<<<<<<<<<<<<<<<<<<<<<<

the Journey to Centennial PASSPORT

ZΦB
CELEBRATING ONE CENTURY · OF SERVICE ·
1920
2020

DATE: ....

EVENT: ....

MOMENT TO REMEMBER: ....

AFFIX STAMP HERE

ZETA PHI BETA SORORITY, INC. <<<<<<
<<<<<<<<<<<<<<<<<<<<<<<<<<<<<<<<<<

9

"I, too, had a dream in the early 1920s of a group of the world's finest women to become sisters of Phi Beta Sigma Fraternity. Thank God I have lived to see my dream come true."
– Honorable Brother Charles Robert Taylor, 1930

PASSPORT
the Journey to **Centennial**

CELEBRATING ONE CENTURY · OF SERVICE · 1920 ZΦB 2020 ™

AFFIX STAMP HERE

DATE: ....

EVENT: ....

MOMENT TO REMEMBER: ....

....

....

....

....

....

....

....

....

....

....

....

....

....

....

<<<<<< ZETA PHI BETA SORORITY, INC.
<<<<<<<<<<<<<<<<<<<<<<<<<<<<<<<<<

CELEBRATING ONE CENTURY · OF SERVICE

1920
ZΦB
2020

the Journey to
Centennial PASSPORT

DATE:_____

EVENT:_____

MOMENT TO REMEMBER:_____

_____

_____

_____

_____

_____

AFFIX STAMP HERE

_____

_____

_____

_____

_____

_____

_____

_____

_____

_____

PASSPORT

the Journey to
Centennial

CELEBRATING ONE CENTURY
1920
ZΦB
2020
OF SERVICE™

AFFIX STAMP HERE

DATE: ....

EVENT: ....

MOMENT TO REMEMBER: ....

....

....

....

....

....

....

....

....

....

....

....

....

....

....

....

12

<<<<<< ZETA PHI BETA SORORITY, INC.
<<<<<<<<<<<<<<<<<<<<<<<<<<<<<<<<

the Journey to Centennial PASSPORT

DATE: ....

EVENT: ....

MOMENT TO REMEMBER: ....

AFFIX STAMP HERE

PASSPORT

the Journey to Centennial

CELEBRATING ONE CENTURY
1920
ZΦB
2020
· OF SERVICE ·

AFFIX STAMP HERE

DATE: ....

EVENT: ....

MOMENT TO REMEMBER: ....

....

....

....

....

....

....

....

....

....

....

....

....

....

....

<<<<<< ZETA PHI BETA SORORITY, INC.
<<<<<<<<<<<<<<<<<<<<<<<<<<<<<<<<<

the Journey to **Centennial** PASSPORT

DATE: ....

EVENT: ....

MOMENT TO REMEMBER: ....

....

....

....

....

....

....

....

....

....

....

....

....

....

....

....

AFFIX STAMP HERE

> "The lamp of learning is passed from hand to hand; the seed maturing
> becomes the many seeds of future plantings."
> – Founder Arizona Cleaver Stemons, 1955

PASSPORT

the Journey to *Centennial*

CELEBRATING ONE CENTURY · OF SERVICE · ZΦB 1920 2020 ™

AFFIX STAMP HERE

DATE: ....

EVENT: ....

MOMENT TO REMEMBER: ....

....

....

....

....

....

....

....

....

....

....

....

....

<<<<<< ZETA PHI BETA SORORITY, INC.
<<<<<<<<<<<<<<<<<<<<<<<<<<<<<<<

CELEBRATING ONE CENTURY · OF SERVICE ·
1920 ZΦB 2020

DATE:_____

EVENT:_____

MOMENT TO REMEMBER:_____

_____

_____

_____

_____

_____

AFFIX STAMP HERE

_____

_____

_____

_____

_____

_____

_____

_____

_____

_____

ZETA PHI BETA SORORITY, INC. <<<<<<
<<<<<<<<<<<<<<<<<<<<<<<<<<<<<<<<

17

PASSPORT

the Journey to
Centennial

CELEBRATING ONE CENTURY
1920
ZΦB
2020
OF SERVICE

AFFIX STAMP HERE

DATE:...

EVENT:...

MOMENT TO REMEMBER:.........

18

<<<<<< ZETA PHI BETA SORORITY, INC.
<<<<<<<<<<<<<<<<<<<<<<<<<<<<<<<<<<

DATE:_____

EVENT:_____

MOMENT TO REMEMBER:_____

_____

_____

_____

_____

_____

_____

_____

_____

_____

_____

_____

_____

_____

_____

_____

AFFIX STAMP HERE

PASSPORT

the Journey to *Centennial*

CELEBRATING ONE CENTURY
1920
ZΦB
2020
OF SERVICE

AFFIX STAMP HERE

DATE:

EVENT:

MOMENT TO REMEMBER:

<<<<<< ZETA PHI BETA SORORITY, INC.
<<<<<<<<<<<<<<<<<<<<<<<<<<<<<

DATE: ....

EVENT: ....

MOMENT TO REMEMBER: ....

AFFIX STAMP HERE

> "We must accept the responsibilities that accompany this achievement, realizing that integration, like democracy, is a great social achievement, not a legacy; therefore, it may not simply be inherited."
> – Dr. Deborah Cannon P. Wolfe, 14th Grand Basileus, 1956

PASSPORT

the Journey to *Centennial*

CELEBRATING ONE CENTURY OF SERVICE
1920
ZΦB
2020

AFFIX STAMP HERE

DATE: ....

EVENT: ....

MOMENT TO REMEMBER: ....

....

....

....

....

....

....

....

....

....

....

....

....

....

....

22

<<<<<< ZETA PHI BETA SORORITY, INC.
<<<<<<<<<<<<<<<<<<<<<<<<<<<<<<<<<

ZΦB
CELEBRATING ONE CENTURY
1920
2020
OF SERVICE

the Journey to
Centennial **PASSPORT**

DATE: ....

EVENT: ....

MOMENT TO REMEMBER: ....

AFFIX STAMP HERE

PASSPORT

the Journey to
Centennial

CELEBRATING ONE CENTURY
1920
ZΦB
2020
· OF SERVICE ·
™

AFFIX STAMP HERE

DATE: _____

EVENT: _____

MOMENT TO REMEMBER: _____

_____

_____

_____

_____

_____

_____

_____

_____

_____

_____

_____

_____

_____

_____

<<<<<< ZETA PHI BETA SORORITY, INC.
<<<<<<<<<<<<<<<<<<<<<<<<<<<<<<<<

the Journey to Centennial PASSPORT

CELEBRATING ONE CENTURY OF SERVICE
1920 ZΦB 2020

DATE: _____

EVENT: _____

MOMENT TO REMEMBER: _____

_____

_____

_____

_____

_____

_____

AFFIX STAMP HERE

_____

_____

_____

_____

_____

_____

_____

_____

_____

"It is that bond of sisterly love in Zeta women that unites us and makes us grow."
- Founder Myrtle Tyler Faithful, 1960

PASSPORT

the Journey to
Centennial

CELEBRATING ONE CENTURY · OF SERVICE · 1920 ZΦB 2020 ™

AFFIX STAMP HERE

DATE: ....

EVENT: ....

MOMENT TO REMEMBER: ....

<<<<<< ZETA PHI BETA SORORITY, INC.
<<<<<<<<<<<<<<<<<<<<<<<<<<<<<<<<<

the *Journey to* **Centennial** PASSPORT

CELEBRATING ONE CENTURY · OF SERVICE · 1920 ZΦB 2020

DATE: ....

EVENT: ....

MOMENT TO REMEMBER: ....

APPLY STAMP HERE

"Those that don't got it, can't show it. Those that got it, can't hide it."
- Soror Zora Neale Hurston, 1903-1960

PASSPORT *the Journey to Centennial*

CELEBRATING ONE CENTURY · OF SERVICE · 1920 ZΦB 2020 ™

AFFIX STAMP HERE

DATE: ....

EVENT: ....

MOMENT TO REMEMBER: ....

....

....

....

....

....

....

....

....

....

....

....

....

28

<<<<<< ZETA PHI BETA SORORITY, INC.
<<<<<<<<<<<<<<<<<<<<<<<<<<<<<<<<<

the Journey to Centennial PASSPORT

ZΦB CELEBRATING ONE CENTURY OF SERVICE 1920 2020

DATE: ....

EVENT: ....

MOMENT TO REMEMBER: ....

AFFIX STAMP HERE

PASSPORT

the Journey to
Centennial

CELEBRATING ONE CENTURY
1920
ZΦB
2020
OF SERVICE ™

AFFIX STAMP HERE

DATE: ....

EVENT: ....

MOMENT TO REMEMBER: ....

<<<<<< ZETA PHI BETA SORORITY, INC.
<<<<<<<<<<<<<<<<<<<<<<<<<<<<<<<<<

DATE:_____

EVENT:_____

MOMENT TO REMEMBER:_____

_____

_____

_____

_____

_____

_____

_____

_____

_____

_____

_____

_____

_____

_____

_____

_____

AFFIX STAMP HERE

On Soror Ida B. King, "She was a parliamentarian of rare talent, an eloquent speaker, and a possessor of "une certaine de chapeaux." - Soror Ola Adams, 1962

PASSPORT
the Journey to *Centennial*

CELEBRATING ONE CENTURY
1920
ZΦB
2020
· OF SERVICE ·

AFFIX STAMP HERE

DATE: ....

EVENT: ....

MOMENT TO REMEMBER: ....

....

....

....

....

....

....

....

....

....

....

....

....

....

<<<<<< ZETA PHI BETA SORORITY, INC.
<<<<<<<<<<<<<<<<<<<<<<<<<<<<<<<<

the Journey to Centennial PASSPORT

CELEBRATING ONE CENTURY OF SERVICE
1920 ZΦB 2020

DATE: _____

EVENT: _____

MOMENT TO REMEMBER: _____

_____

_____

_____

_____

_____

AFFIX STAMP HERE

_____

_____

_____

_____

_____

_____

_____

_____

_____

_____

ZETA PHI BETA SORORITY, INC. <<<<<<
<<<<<<<<<<<<<<<<<<<<<<<<<<<<<<<<<<

33

PASSPORT

the Journey to
Centennial

CELEBRATING ONE CENTURY
1920 ΖΦΒ 2020
· OF SERVICE ·

AFFIX STAMP HERE

DATE: _____

EVENT: _____

MOMENT TO REMEMBER: _____

_____
_____
_____
_____
_____
_____
_____
_____
_____
_____
_____
_____
_____
_____

<<<<<< ZETA PHI BETA SORORITY, INC.
<<<<<<<<<<<<<<<<<<<<<<<<<<<<<<<

the Journey to Centennial PASSPORT

CELEBRATING ONE CENTURY OF SERVICE 1920 ZΦB 2020

DATE: ....

EVENT: ....

MOMENT TO REMEMBER: ....

AFFIX STAMP HERE

"Wherever I went and whatever I did, I was always aware that
consciously or unconsciously someone was saying, 'That's Zeta Phi Beta Sorority'."
- Soror Isabel Morgan Herson, 16th Grand Basileus, 1970

PASSPORT

the Journey to
Centennial

CELEBRATING ONE CENTURY
1920
ZΦB
2020
OF SERVICE

AFFIX STAMP HERE

DATE: ....

EVENT: ....

MOMENT TO REMEMBER: ....

....

....

....

....

....

....

....

....

....

....

....

....

....

....

....

....

<<<<<< ZETA PHI BETA SORORITY, INC.
<<<<<<<<<<<<<<<<<<<<<<<<<<<<<<<<<

the Journey to Centennial PASSPORT

CELEBRATING ONE CENTURY OF SERVICE 1920 ZΦB 2020

DATE: _____

EVENT: _____

MOMENT TO REMEMBER: _____

_____

_____

_____

_____

_____

_____

_____

_____

_____

_____

_____

_____

_____

_____

_____

_____

AFFIX STAMP HERE

PASSPORT

the Journey to **Centennial**

CELEBRATING ONE CENTURY OF SERVICE
1920
ZΦB
2020

AFFIX STAMP HERE

DATE: _____

EVENT: _____

MOMENT TO REMEMBER: _____

_____

_____

_____

_____

_____

_____

_____

_____

_____

_____

_____

_____

_____

38

<<<<<< ZETA PHI BETA SORORITY, INC.
<<<<<<<<<<<<<<<<<<<<<<<<<<<<<<<

the Journey to *Centennial* **PASSPORT**

DATE: ....

EVENT: ....

MOMENT TO REMEMBER: ....

AFFIX STAMP HERE

"Zeta Phi Beta Sorority, Inc. ... a Community-Conscious, Action-Oriented Organization."
- Dr. Janice Gantt Kissner, 17th Grand Basileus, 1975

PASSPORT *the Journey to Centennial*

AFFIX STAMP HERE

DATE:_____

EVENT:_____

MOMENT TO REMEMBER:_____

_____

_____

_____

_____

_____

_____

_____

_____

_____

_____

_____

_____

_____

_____

<<<<<< ZETA PHI BETA SORORITY, INC.
<<<<<<<<<<<<<<<<<<<<<<<<<<<<<<<

the Journey to Centennial PASSPORT

CELEBRATING ONE CENTURY OF SERVICE
ZΦB 1920 2020

DATE: _____

EVENT: _____

MOMENT TO REMEMBER: _____

_____

_____

_____

_____

_____

_____

_____

_____

_____

_____

_____

_____

_____

_____

AFFIX STAMP HERE

PASSPORT

the Journey to
Centennial

CELEBRATING ONE CENTURY · OF SERVICE
1920 ZΦB 2020

AFFIX STAMP HERE

DATE: _____

EVENT: _____

MOMENT TO REMEMBER: _____

<<<<<< ZETA PHI BETA SORORITY, INC.
<<<<<<<<<<<<<<<<<<<<<<<<<<<<<<<<<

DATE: _____

EVENT: _____

MOMENT TO REMEMBER: _____

AFFIX STAMP HERE

PASSPORT

the Journey to
Centennial

CELEBRATING ONE CENTURY
1920
ZΦB
2020
- OF SERVICE -

AFFIX STAMP HERE

DATE: _____

EVENT: _____

MOMENT TO REMEMBER: _____

_____
_____
_____
_____
_____
_____
_____
_____
_____
_____
_____
_____
_____

<<<<<< ZETA PHI BETA SORORITY, INC.
<<<<<<<<<<<<<<<<<<<<<<<<<<<<<<<<

the Journey to Centennial PASSPORT

ZΦB · CELEBRATING ONE CENTURY · 1920 2020 · OF SERVICE ™

DATE: _____

EVENT: _____

MOMENT TO REMEMBER: _____

_____

_____

_____

_____

_____

AFFIX STAMP HERE

_____

_____

_____

_____

_____

_____

_____

_____

_____

_____

PASSPORT

the Journey to
Centennial

CELEBRATING ONE CENTURY
1920
ZΦB
2020
OF SERVICE

AFFIX STAMP HERE

DATE: _____

EVENT: _____

MOMENT TO REMEMBER: _____

_____

_____

_____

_____

_____

_____

_____

_____

_____

_____

_____

_____

_____

<<<<<< ZETA PHI BETA SORORITY, INC.
<<<<<<<<<<<<<<<<<<<<<<<<<<<<<<<<<

CELEBRATING ONE CENTURY OF SERVICE

1920 ZΦB 2020

DATE: _____

EVENT: _____

MOMENT TO REMEMBER: _____

_____

_____

_____

_____

_____

AFFIX STAMP HERE

_____

_____

_____

_____

_____

_____

_____

_____

_____

_____

_____

> "No other issue should be of more critical importance to each and every member of the African American community than the crisis affecting our African American males."
> – Dr. Eunice S. Thomas, 19th Grand Basileus, 1990

PASSPORT
the Journey to **Centennial**

CELEBRATING ONE CENTURY
1920
ΖΦΒ
2020
OF SERVICE

AFFIX STAMP HERE

DATE: ....

EVENT: ....

MOMENT TO REMEMBER: ....

....

....

....

....

....

....

....

....

....

....

....

....

....

....

....

<<<<<< ZETA PHI BETA SORORITY, INC.
<<<<<<<<<<<<<<<<<<<<<<<<<<<<<<<

DATE: ....

EVENT: ....

MOMENT TO REMEMBER: ....

AFFIX STAMP HERE

PASSPORT

the Journey to
Centennial

CELEBRATING ONE CENTURY
ZΦB
1920
2020
OF SERVICE

AFFIX STAMP HERE

DATE: ....

EVENT: ....

MOMENT TO REMEMBER: ....

....

....

....

....

....

....

....

....

....

....

....

....

....

....

....

....

<<<<<< ZETA PHI BETA SORORITY, INC.
<<<<<<<<<<<<<<<<<<<<<<<<<<<<<<<<<<<

DATE: _____

EVENT: _____

MOMENT TO REMEMBER: _____

_____

_____

_____

_____

_____

_____

_____

_____

_____

_____

_____

_____

_____

_____

_____

_____

AFFIX STAMP HERE

PASSPORT

the Journey to **Centennial**

CELEBRATING ONE CENTURY
1920
ZΦB
2020
OF SERVICE

AFFIX STAMP HERE

DATE:

EVENT:

MOMENT TO REMEMBER:

<<<<<< ZETA PHI BETA SORORITY, INC.
<<<<<<<<<<<<<<<<<<<<<<<<<<<<<<

the Journey to Centennial PASSPORT

DATE: ....

EVENT: ....

MOMENT TO REMEMBER: ....

AFFIX STAMP HERE

"Soar on, Sweet Zeta! Ride the White Dove as it lifts its wings in its flight of love."
- Soror Nancy Shepard, 1996, 75th Anniversary Celebration

PASSPORT

the Journey to *Centennial*

CELEBRATING ONE CENTURY
1920
ZΦB
2020
OF SERVICE

AFFIX STAMP HERE

DATE:_____

EVENT:_____

MOMENT TO REMEMBER:_____

_____

_____

_____

_____

_____

_____

_____

_____

_____

_____

_____

_____

_____

_____

_____

_____

<<<<<< ZETA PHI BETA SORORITY, INC.
<<<<<<<<<<<<<<<<<<<<<<<<<<<<<<<<<<

![Celebrating One Century of Service 1920-2020 ZΦB] the *Journey to* **Centennial** PASSPORT

DATE: _____

EVENT: _____

MOMENT TO REMEMBER: _____

_____

_____

_____

_____

_____

_____

AFFIX STAMP HERE

_____

_____

_____

_____

_____

_____

_____

_____

_____

_____

ZETA PHI BETA SORORITY, INC. <<<<<<
<<<<<<<<<<<<<<<<<<<<<<<<<<<<<<<<<<

55

PASSPORT

the Journey to
Centennial

CELEBRATING ONE CENTURY
1920
ZΦB
2020
OF SERVICE

AFFIX STAMP HERE

DATE:_____

EVENT:_____

MOMENT TO REMEMBER:_____

<<<<<< ZETA PHI BETA SORORITY, INC.
<<<<<<<<<<<<<<<<<<<<<<<<<<<<<<

the Journey to Centennial PASSPORT

CELEBRATING ONE CENTURY OF SERVICE
ZΦB 1920 2020

DATE: ....

EVENT: ....

MOMENT TO REMEMBER: ....

AFFIX STAMP HERE

ZETA PHI BETA SORORITY, INC. <<<<<<
<<<<<<<<<<<<<<<<<<<<<<<<<<<<<<<<<<

57

PASSPORT

the Journey to
Centennial

CELEBRATING ONE CENTURY
1920
ZΦB
2020
OF SERVICE

AFFIX STAMP HERE

DATE: _____

EVENT: _____

MOMENT TO REMEMBER: _____

_____

_____

_____

_____

_____

_____

_____

_____

_____

_____

_____

_____

_____

_____

_____

_____

_____

<<<<<< ZETA PHI BETA SORORITY, INC.
<<<<<<<<<<<<<<<<<<<<<<<<<<<<<<<<

the Journey to Centennial PASSPORT

CELEBRATING ONE CENTURY OF SERVICE
1920 ZΦB 2020

DATE: _____

EVENT: _____

MOMENT TO REMEMBER: _____

_____

_____

_____

_____

_____

_____

_____

_____

_____

_____

_____

_____

_____

_____

_____

_____

AFFIX STAMP HERE

PASSPORT

the Journey to
Centennial

CELEBRATING ONE CENTURY
1920
ZΦB
2020
OF SERVICE

AFFIX STAMP HERE

DATE: ....

EVENT: ....

MOMENT TO REMEMBER: ....

....

....

....

....

....

....

....

....

....

....

....

....

....

....

....

60

<<<<<< ZETA PHI BETA SORORITY, INC.
<<<<<<<<<<<<<<<<<<<<<<<<<<<<<<<

the Journey to Centennial PASSPORT

CELEBRATING ONE CENTURY OF SERVICE
1920 ZΦB 2020

DATE: ....

EVENT: ....

MOMENT TO REMEMBER: ....

....

....

....

....

....

AFFIX STAMP HERE

....

....

....

....

....

....

....

....

....

....

....

PASSPORT

the Journey to Centennial

CELEBRATING ONE CENTURY
1920 ZΦB 2020
OF SERVICE

AFFIX STAMP HERE

DATE: ....

EVENT: ....

MOMENT TO REMEMBER: ....

....

....

....

....

....

....

....

....

....

....

....

<<<<<< ZETA PHI BETA SORORITY, INC.
<<<<<<<<<<<<<<<<<<<<<<<<<<<<<<<<

CELEBRATING ONE CENTURY OF SERVICE
1920 ZΦB 2020

DATE:_____

EVENT:_____

MOMENT TO REMEMBER:_____

_____

_____

_____

_____

_____

AFFIX STAMP HERE

_____

_____

_____

_____

_____

_____

_____

_____

_____

_____

PASSPORT

the Journey to Centennial

CELEBRATING ONE CENTURY
1920 ZΦB 2020
OF SERVICE ™

AFFIX STAMP HERE

DATE:..................................

EVENT:................................

MOMENT TO REMEMBER:.........

_____

_____

_____

_____

_____

_____

_____

_____

_____

_____

_____

_____

_____

_____

_____

_____

64

<<<<<< ZETA PHI BETA SORORITY, INC.
<<<<<<<<<<<<<<<<<<<<<<<<<<<<<<<<<

CELEBRATING ONE CENTURY · OF SERVICE

1920 ZΦB 2020

DATE: ....

EVENT: ....

MOMENT TO REMEMBER: ....

....

....

....

....

....

....

....

....

....

....

....

....

....

....

....

....

....

AFFIX STAMP HERE

PASSPORT

the Journey to
Centennial

CELEBRATING ONE CENTURY
1920
ZΦB
2020
OF SERVICE
™

AFFIX STAMP HERE

DATE:_____

EVENT:_____

MOMENT TO REMEMBER:_____

_____

_____

_____

_____

_____

_____

_____

_____

_____

_____

_____

_____

_____

_____

<<<<<< ZETA PHI BETA SORORITY, INC.
<<<<<<<<<<<<<<<<<<<<<<<<<<<<<<<<<

ZΦB
CELEBRATING ONE CENTURY
1920
2020
OF SERVICE ™

the Journey to **Centennial** PASSPORT

DATE: _____

EVENT: _____

MOMENT TO REMEMBER: _____

_____

_____

_____

_____

_____

_____

_____

_____

_____

_____

_____

AFFIX STAMP HERE

_____

_____

_____

ORORITY, INC. <<<<<<
<<<<<<<<<<<<<<<<<<<<<

67

PASSPORT

the Journey to
Centennial

CELEBRATING ONE CENTURY
1920
ZΦB
2020
OF SERVICE

AFFIX STAMP HERE

DATE: _____

EVENT: _____

MOMENT TO REMEMBER: _____

_____
_____
_____
_____
_____
_____

_____
_____
_____
_____
_____
_____
_____

68

<<<<<< ZETA PHI BETA SORORITY
<<<<<<<<<<<<<<<<<<<<<<<<<<

the Journey to Centennial PASSPORT

CELEBRATING ONE CENTURY OF SERVICE
1920 ZΦB 2020

DATE: _____

EVENT: _____

MOMENT TO REMEMBER: _____

AFFIX STAMP HERE

ZETA PHI BETA SORORITY, INC. <<<<<<
<<<<<<<<<<<<<<<<<<<<<<<<<<<<<<<<<

69

"The oath you took did not make you a Zeta, it made you a member;
but how you live that oath is what makes you a Zeta!"
- Soror Mary Breaux Wright, 24th International Grand Basileus, 2012

PASSPORT *the Journey to Centennial*

CELEBRATING ONE CENTURY
1920 ZΦB 2020
OF SERVICE

AFFIX STAMP HERE

DATE: ....

EVENT: ....

MOMENT TO REMEMBER: ....

....

....

....

....

....

....

....

....

....

....

....

....

....

....

<<<<<< ZETA PHI BETA SORORITY, INC.
<<<<<<<<<<<<<<<<<<<<<<<<<<<<<<<

CELEBRATING ONE CENTURY OF SERVICE
ZΦB
1920 2020

DATE: ....

EVENT: ....

MOMENT TO REMEMBER: ....

AFFIX STAMP HERE

PASSPORT

the Journey to
Centennial

CELEBRATING ONE CENTURY
1920
ZΦB
2020
OF SERVICE

AFFIX STAMP HERE

DATE: _____

EVENT: _____

MOMENT TO REMEMBER: _____

_____

_____

_____

_____

_____

_____

_____

_____

_____

_____

_____

_____

<<<<<< ZETA PHI BETA SORORITY, INC.
<<<<<<<<<<<<<<<<<<<<<<<<<<<<<<<

DATE: _____

EVENT: _____

MOMENT TO REMEMBER: _____

_____

_____

_____

_____

_____

AFFIX STAMP HERE

_____

_____

_____

_____

_____

_____

_____

_____

_____

_____

_____

> "A walk around the reservoir of Howard University in 1919 would unfold the vision of a brother-sister bond that has changed the lives of thousands throughout the world for nearly 100 years."
> — Honorable Brother Jonathan A. Mason, Sr., 34th International President, Phi Beta Sigma Fraternity, Inc. Centennial President

PASSPORT
the Journey to
Centennial

CELEBRATING ONE CENTURY
1920
ZΦB
2020
OF SERVICE

AFFIX STAMP HERE

DATE: ....

EVENT: ....

MOMENT TO REMEMBER: ....

_____

_____

_____

_____

_____

_____

_____

_____

_____

_____

_____

_____

_____

<<<<<< ZETA PHI BETA SORORITY, INC.
<<<<<<<<<<<<<<<<<<<<<<<<<<<<<<<<<

the Journey to Centennial PASSPORT

DATE: ....

EVENT: ....

MOMENT TO REMEMBER: ....

APPIX STAMP HERE

PASSPORT

the Journey to **Centennial**

CELEBRATING ONE CENTURY
1920
ZΦB
2020
OF SERVICE

AFFIX STAMP HERE

DATE: ....

EVENT: ....

MOMENT TO REMEMBER: ....

....

....

....

....

....

....

....

....

....

....

....

....

....

....

<<<<<< ZETA PHI BETA SORORITY, INC.
<<<<<<<<<<<<<<<<<<<<<<<<<<<<<<<<<

the Journey to Centennial PASSPORT

ZΦB · CELEBRATING ONE CENTURY OF SERVICE · 1920 2020

DATE: _____

EVENT: _____

MOMENT TO REMEMBER: _____

_____

_____

_____

_____

_____

AFFIX STAMP HERE

_____

_____

_____

_____

_____

_____

_____

_____

_____

What will I do to "Be Finer in 2020"?

PASSPORT

the Journey to
Centennial

CELEBRATING ONE CENTURY
1920
ZΦB
2020
OF SERVICE

DATE: _____

EVENT: _____

MOMENT TO REMEMBER: _____

AFFIX STAMP HERE

<<<<<< ZETA PHI BETA SORORITY, INC.
<<<<<<<<<<<<<<<<<<<<<<<<<<<<<<<<

ZΦB

CELEBRATING ONE CENTURY
1920
2020
OF SERVICE

the Journey to
Centennial PASSPORT

DATE:..

EVENT:...

MOMENT TO REMEMBER:..........

PASSPORT
the Journey to Centennial

CELEBRATING ONE CENTURY OF SERVICE
1920 ΖΦΒ 2020

AFFIX STAMP HERE

DATE: _____

EVENT: _____

MOMENT TO REMEMBER: _____

_____

_____

_____

_____

_____

_____

_____

_____

_____

_____

_____

_____

_____

<<<<<< ZETA PHI BETA SORORITY, INC.
<<<<<<<<<<<<<<<<<<<<<<<<<<<<<<<<

DATE: _____

EVENT: _____

MOMENT TO REMEMBER: _____

_____

_____

_____

_____

AFFIX STAMP HERE

_____

_____

_____

_____

_____

_____

_____

_____

_____

_____

PASSPORT

the Journey to *Centennial*

CELEBRATING ONE CENTURY
1920
ZΦB
2020
OF SERVICE

AFFIX STAMP HERE

DATE: ....

EVENT: ....

MOMENT TO REMEMBER: ....

<<<<<< ZETA PHI BETA SORORITY, INC.
<<<<<<<<<<<<<<<<<<<<<<<<<<<<<<<

![Zeta Phi Beta Sorority Centennial Passport]

the Journey to Centennial PASSPORT

DATE: _____

EVENT: _____

MOMENT TO REMEMBER: _____

_____

_____

_____

_____

AFFIX STAMP HERE

_____

_____

_____

_____

_____

_____

_____

_____

_____

_____

_____

PASSPORT

the Journey to
Centennial

CELEBRATING ONE CENTURY · OF SERVICE ·
1920 ZΦB 2020

AFFIX STAMP HERE

DATE: _____

EVENT: _____

MOMENT TO REMEMBER: _____

_____

_____

_____

_____

_____

_____

_____

_____

_____

_____

_____

_____

_____

<<<<<< ZETA PHI BETA SORORITY, INC.
<<<<<<<<<<<<<<<<<<<<<<<<<<<<<<<

the Journey to Centennial PASSPORT

DATE: ....

EVENT: ....

MOMENT TO REMEMBER: ....

Who will I connect with as I travel the highways reflected in
"The House by the Side of the Road"?

PASSPORT

the Journey to
Centennial

CELEBRATING ONE CENTURY
1920
ZΦB
2020
OF SERVICE ™

AFFIX STAMP HERE

DATE: ....

EVENT: ....

MOMENT TO REMEMBER: ....

....

....

....

....

....

....

....

....

....

....

....

....

....

....

<<<<<< ZETA PHI BETA SORORITY, INC.
<<<<<<<<<<<<<<<<<<<<<<<<<<<<<<<<

the Journey to Centennial PASSPORT

CELEBRATING ONE CENTURY OF SERVICE
ZΦB 1920 2020

DATE:..

EVENT:..

MOMENT TO REMEMBER:.........

AFFIX STAMP HERE

PASSPORT

the Journey to
Centennial

CELEBRATING ONE CENTURY
· OF SERVICE ·
1920 ΖΦΒ 2020 ™

AFFIX STAMP HERE

DATE: ....

EVENT: ....

MOMENT TO REMEMBER: ....

....

....

....

....

....

....

....

....

....

....

....

....

<<<<<< ZETA PHI BETA SORORITY, INC.
<<<<<<<<<<<<<<<<<<<<<<<<<<<<<<<<<

DATE: ....

EVENT: ....

MOMENT TO REMEMBER: ....

_____

_____

_____

_____

_____

_____

_____

_____

_____

_____

_____

_____

_____

APPLY STAMP HERE

When will I experience my transformation as a next level community-conscious, action-oriented member?

PASSPORT *the Journey to* *Centennial*

CELEBRATING ONE CENTURY
1920
ZΦB
2020
OF SERVICE

AFFIX STAMP HERE

DATE:_____

EVENT:_____

MOMENT TO REMEMBER:_____

_____

_____

_____

_____

_____

_____

_____

_____

_____

_____

_____

_____

<<<<<< ZETA PHI BETA SORORITY, INC.
<<<<<<<<<<<<<<<<<<<<<<<<<<<<<<<<<

CELEBRATING ONE CENTURY
1920
ZΦB
2020
OF SERVICE

DATE: ....

EVENT: ....

MOMENT TO REMEMBER: ......

AFFIX STAMP HERE

INC. <<<<<<
<<<<<<<<<<

91

PASSPORT

the Journey to
Centennial

CELEBRATING ONE CENTURY · OF SERVICE
1920
ZΦB
2020

AFFIX STAMP HERE

DATE:

EVENT:

MOMENT TO REMEMBER:

<<<<<< ZETA PHI BETA SOR
<<<<<<<<<<<<<<<<<<

CELEBRATING ONE CENTURY OF SERVICE
1920 ZΦB 2020

the Journey to *Centennial* PASSPORT

DATE: ....

EVENT: ....

MOMENT TO REMEMBER: ....

AFFIX STAMP HERE

ZETA PHI BETA SORORITY, INC. <<<<<<
<<<<<<<<<<<<<<<<<<<<<<<<<<<<<<<<<

93

How will Zeta be a stronger organization because of my personal commitment to Service, Scholarship, Sisterhood and Finer Womanhood?

PASSPORT

the Journey to *Centennial*

CELEBRATING ONE CENTURY
1920
ZΦB
2020
OF SERVICE

AFFIX STAMP HERE

DATE:_____

EVENT:_____

MOMENT TO REMEMBER:_____

_____

_____

_____

_____

_____

_____

_____

_____

_____

_____

_____

_____

_____

<<<<<< ZETA PHI BETA SORORITY, INC.
<<<<<<<<<<<<<<<<<<<<<<<<<<<<<<<<<

the Journey to Centennial PASSPORT

CELEBRATING ONE CENTURY OF SERVICE
1920 · ZΦB · 2020

DATE:_____

EVENT:_____

MOMENT TO REMEMBER:_____

_____

_____

_____

_____

_____

_____

_____

_____

_____

_____

_____

_____

_____

_____

_____

AFFIX STAMP HERE

PASSPORT

the Journey to **Centennial**

CELEBRATING ONE CENTURY OF SERVICE

1920 ZΦB 2020

AFFIX STAMP HERE

DATE: ....

EVENT: ....

MOMENT TO REMEMBER: ....

....

....

....

....

....

....

....

....

....

....

....

....

....

....

....

....

<<<<<< ZETA PHI BETA SORORITY, INC.
<<<<<<<<<<<<<<<<<<<<<<<<<<<<<<<<<

the Journey to Centennial PASSPORT

CELEBRATING ONE CENTURY · OF SERVICE
1920 ZΦB 2020

ZΦB

DATE: _____

EVENT: _____

MOMENT TO REMEMBER: _____

_____

_____

_____

_____

_____

_____

_____

_____

_____

_____

_____

_____

_____

_____

AFFIX STAMP HERE

ZETA PHI BETA SORORITY, INC. <<<<<<
<<<<<<<<<<<<<<<<<<<<<<<<<<<<<<<<<<<

PASSPORT

the Journey to **Centennial**

CELEBRATING ONE CENTURY · OF SERVICE
1920 ZΦB 2020

AFFIX STAMP HERE

DATE:_____

EVENT:_____

MOMENT TO REMEMBER:_____

_____

_____

_____

_____

_____

_____

_____

_____

_____

_____

_____

_____

_____

_____

_____

<<<<<< ZETA PHI BETA SORORITY, INC.
<<<<<<<<<<<<<<<<<<<<<<<<<<<<<<<<<<

the Journey to Centennial PASSPORT

DATE: _____

EVENT: _____

MOMENT TO REMEMBER: _____

_____

_____

_____

_____

_____

_____

_____

_____

_____

_____

_____

_____

_____

_____

_____

AFFIX STAMP HERE

PASSPORT

the Journey to
Centennial

CELEBRATING ONE CENTURY
1920
ZΦB
2020
· OF SERVICE ·

AFFIX STAMP HERE

DATE: ....

EVENT: ....

MOMENT TO REMEMBER: ....

....

....

....

....

....

....

....

....

....

....

....

....

....

....

100

<<<<<< ZETA PHI BETA SORORITY, INC.
<<<<<<<<<<<<<<<<<<<<<<<<<<<<<<<<<<

Dr. Jylla Moore Tearte
20th International Grand Basileus
Centennial Commission Chair

Soror Denise Marie Snow
Centennial Passport Chair

Soror Amber Pratcher
Compilation of Photos

Soror Doris McAdams Stokes
Compilation of Quotes

Additional Notes:

Additional Notes:

Additional Notes:

Additional Notes:

Additional Notes:

Additional Notes:

Additional Notes:

Additional Notes:

Additional Notes:

www.ingramcontent.com/pod-product-compliance
Lightning Source LLC
Chambersburg PA
CBHW050241290326
41930CB00043B/3182